# Plastics

**Ruth Thomson**

Photography by Neil Thomson

## W

### FRANKLIN WATTS
LONDON • SYDNEY

First published in 2006 by
Franklin Watts
338 Euston Road
London NW1 3BH

Franklin Watts Australia
Hachette Children's Books
Level 17/207 Kent Street
Sydney NSW 2000

Text copyright © Ruth Thomson 2006
Photographs © Neil Thomson 2006

Editor: Rachel Cooke
Design: Holly Mann
Art Director: Rachel Hamdi
Consultant: Dr Mercia Gick, British Plastics
Federation

**Additional photography**
Thanks are due to the following for kind
permission to reproduce photographs:
Franklin Watts 6cr, 6bl, 7, 8tr, 9tr, 10tr, 11cr,
13br, 19cl, 19bl, 23tl, 23cl, 24bl, 25tr, 25tl;
Recycle now 11l, 11tr, 11cl, 12l,
19tr, 22cr; Jenny Matthews 18r, 21b; Smile
Plastics 26b, 27b; Sankey Plastics 26t.

ISBN 0 7496 6101 1

A CIP catalogue record for this
book is available from the
British Library.

Dewey Decimal Classification
Number: 668.41

Printed in China

**Acknowledgements**
The author and publisher wish to thank the
following people for their help with this book:
Monique Fagin, Wally Petersen, Yandiswe,
Irvine, Vukile and Felicity at *Kommetjie
Environmental Awareness Group (KEAG)*;
Gladys King and Nobulele Simanga (*Circle
Waste Craft*; South Africa) Braam and Daleen
Muller (*NUTU*); Steven Cheetham (*Atlantic
Plastics*, Cape Town); Hugh Willis (*Blowplas*,
Cape Town); Nelson Lombardi B. Cruz
(*Engeplas*, Brazil); Unifil, Brazil; Carla Mocellin
(*Aguas Ouro Fino*, Brazil); Colin Williamson
(*Smile Plastics*); Vinod Kumar Sharma,
Yole Milani Medeiros, Cintia Cimbaluk,
Joina Almeida, Osama Ali, Sue Adler
and Mark Watson.

# Contents

What are plastics like?    6

Making plastic    8

Saving plastic    10

Re-using plastic    12

Junk or treasure?    14

Too good to throw away    16

Plastic bags    18

Bags of ideas    20

Recycling plastics    22

New plastic from old    24

Fantastic plastic    26

Glossary    28

Guess what?    29

Useful websites    29

Index    30

Words printed in **bold** are explained in the glossary.

# What are plastics like?

Plastics are a very useful modern **material**. They can be made into any shape – including hollow containers, long tubes, flat sheets or thin **fibres**. Many plastics are colourful, others are white or see-through.

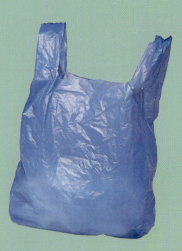

Some plastics are hard, stiff and strong. They can be shaped to make sturdy things such as bowls, boxes, buckets, furniture and dustbins.

Some plastics are soft, thin and squashy. They can be stretched, rolled or folded. Soft plastics are used to make bags, shower curtains or food wrapping.

6

Plastic is very light compared with glass or metal.

Many bottles are made of plastic. They are lighter to transport than glass ones and do not break if you drop them.

**Plastics are waterproof.** They do not let water in or out.

Outdoor equipment is often made of plastic, because it does not **rot** like wood or **rust** like steel in wet weather.

## LOOK AND SEE

*How many things can you find at home or at school made of plastic?*

*If there were no plastic, what materials might these things be made of instead?*

## Wish-wash

Plastic things are easy to keep clean. They do not stain or mark easily. They last a long time.

# Making plastic

Some plastics are made from **natural materials**, but most are made from **chemicals** in **crude oil**. The oil is heated so that it separates. The lightest oil is used to make plastic **granules**. These are sent to **factories** which make them into products.

## Melting and moulding

The plastic is heated until it melts into a syrupy **liquid**. This can be shaped in a **mould**. As it cools, the plastic hardens into the shape of the mould. There are many different ways of moulding plastic.

Bottles can be made in different shapes, sizes and colours.

## Squeezed

It can be squeezed through a hole to make a long tube. Hosepipes are made like this.

## Blown

It can blown into a mould to make a hollow object. The mould looks like the outside of the object. Bottles are made like this.

## Poured

It can be poured into a mould to make a solid object, such as paperweights.

## Pushed

Plastic can also be pushed under pressure through a narrow tube into a mould. This is the most common way of moulding plastics. Bowls and buckets are made like this.

### LOOK AND SEE

*Look on the bottom of a bowl or tub. You will see a bump in the centre. This is where the plastic was cut from the end of the tube.*

## Sheets and bags

To make plastic sheets, plastic is formed into a tube.

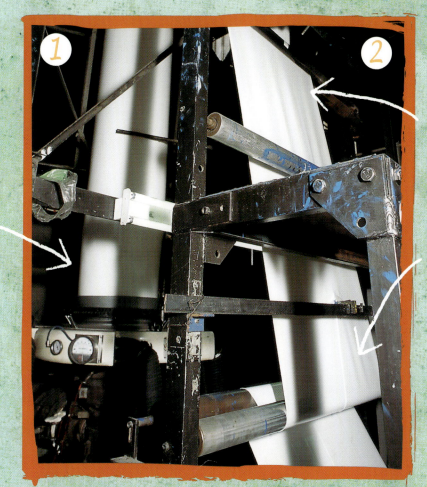

1. A jet of air blows the tube up like a balloon.

2. A series of rollers stretch and then flatten the plastic into thin sheets.

# Saving plastic

People often throw away plastic **packaging**, such as bottles, tubs or wrapping after only one use. These fill up **landfill sites**, because they do not rot easily. Some plastics can be burned as fuel to provide heat and electricity, but we need to be more careful with plastic.

## Ready refills

This biker is delivering large bottles of water to offices. When the bottles are empty, he will collect them so they can be refilled.

## Anyone for oil?

In Morocco, traders go from house to house refilling empty cooking oil bottles.

## Assorted sweets

This shop in Egypt **re-uses** clear plastic CD holders to display sweets.

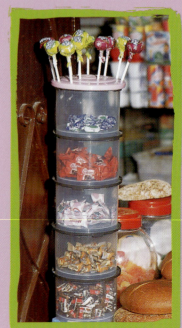

# YOU CAN HELP

Find ways to use less plastic.

## REDUCE

Persuade your family to:

- buy refill sachets instead of new bottles of detergent.

- pick loose fruit and vegetables rather than ones pre-packed in plastic boxes.

- choose plastic containers that can be **recycled**. These will usually have a sign like this.

- buy goods with as little plastic packaging as possible or in re-usable containers.

## RE-USE

- Keep containers with lids as storage boxes.

- Wash and re-use plastic plates and cutlery.

- Plant seeds in yoghurt pots, food trays or egg boxes.

- If you take a packed lunch to school, put food in a lunchbox and drink in a re-usable bottle.

## RECYCLE

- Wash and squash plastic bottles and remove the caps. Put the bottles into a recycling bank or leave them out for recycling collection.

# Re-using plastic

People have thought of clever ways to re-use plastic things instead of throwing them away.

## A bird scarer

A CD on a string twists and glints in a vegetable garden to scare away any hungry birds.

## A shiny lampshade

Several CDs glued together make up this lampshade. Light glows through the holes as well as from underneath.

## A musical handbag

Two old records sewn onto a piece of inner tube from a truck tyre make an original handbag.

## Made for sweeping

This brush and broom are made of strips cut from plastic water bottles.

Brush

Broom

## A soap dish

The upturned base of a plastic bottle has been turned into a soap dish.

## A perfect paint palette

Bottle caps become paint holders set into a hardboard palette.

YOUR TURN

*What could you make with an old plastic bottle?*

## A model

*You could make a model.*

## A rain gauge

*You could cut a bottle in two and upturn the top half inside the bottom half to make a rain gauge.*

*Use this outside to measure how much rainfall there is.*

# Junk or treasure?

In South Africa, unemployed people were paid to clean up beaches. Most of the rubbish was plastic and was sent straight to landfill sites. One group decided to earn money by making things with the waste they found.

## Bright beads

People string bottle caps and pieces of plastic hosepipe onto old rope to make bead curtains.

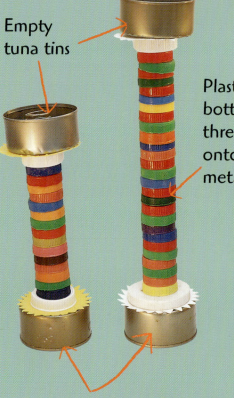

Empty tuna tins

Plastic bottle caps threaded onto a metal rod

Tuna tins filled with cement to make a solid base

## Crazy candlesticks

They also make unusual candlesticks with bottle caps.

Stars cut from plastic bottles

A washing powder ball

A star fixed to a bottle cap

## Christmas tree decorations

The group also creates unusual Christmas tree decorations.

## Junky jewellery

They make plastic jewellery, too.

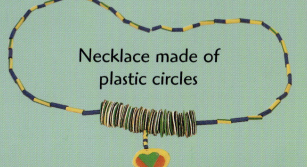

Necklace made of plastic circles

15

*Make a collection of different coloured bottle caps.*

*Use them as games pieces for noughts and crosses, solitaire, draughts or other board games.*

Solitaire

# Plastic bags

In the past people took their own bags or baskets when they went shopping. Now shops provide plastic bags. These are cheap, light and strong, but people often throw them away carelessly.

## A sign of the times

Billions of flimsy bags end up as rubbish after a single shopping trip. In many places, these blow around city streets, clog drains and waterways, litter beaches and choke animals. Many countries are now encouraging people to use fewer bags.

## Bag ban

In Bangladesh, plastic bags blocked storm drains, causing flooding, so the government banned them. Now people shop with cloth bags woven from **jute**.

# A bag for life

Many supermarkets sell large, strong shopping bags for people to use every time they shop. Other supermarkets offer a small refund if you bring your own bags or charge extra if you use theirs.

### REFUSE

- *Say NO to a plastic bag if you buy something small or easy to carry.*

### REDUCE

- *Encourage your family to use a cloth bag, a basket, box or trolley for their shopping. Design your own logo for a cloth bag.*

- *Avoid putting things with handles into bags.*

- *Count how many plastic bags your family uses each week. Can you reduce the number week by week?*

- *Buy rubbish bags and bin liners made from recycled plastic.*

### RE-USE

- *Keep used plastic bags together in a handy place. Re-use them for shopping or storage.*

- *Give clean, unwanted plastic bags to charity shops.*

# Bags of ideas

Thrown-away plastic bags are a useful free raw material for craftspeople without a great deal of money.

## Crochet crafts

1. This South African craftswoman cuts a plastic bag into a long, narrow, continuous strip.

2. She **crochets** the strip with a hook, to create a hat, a handbag or a basket.

These two craftswomen display some of the things that they have made from plastic bags.

## Colourful chickens

Some years ago, a group of South Africans made funny chickens from discarded supermarket plastic bags and wire. They sold them on the street to passers-by and tourists.

Now people in South Africa have to pay for supermarket bags, so thrown-away ones are harder to find. The craftsmen buy cheap recycled plastic sheeting from factories. They use this to make all sorts of different animals.

## What a ball!

Children in Africa cannot always afford to buy footballs, so they make their own. They squash old plastic bags into a ball shape and skilfully tie them tightly together with knotted plastic strips.

# Recycling plastics

Almost all plastics can be recycled. Most recyclable plastics come from packaging, especially bottles and see-through film.

## Recycling bottles

1. People sort bottles by type and colour. Different types can not be recycled together, as they melt at different temperatures.

2. Each type is squashed and tied into a **bale** to transport to a plastics factory. At the factory, a grinder chops up the bottles into tiny **flakes.**

3. The flakes are washed, dried and then melted. The soft plastic is pushed through a screen and comes out in long strings. After cooling these are chopped into **pellets**, which factories buy for making new products.

## LOOK AND SEE

Most plastics have long names. The names of the seven major types have been shortened and given a number. Look on plastic objects for a number. It helps people sort plastic for recycling.

**1 PET**

*Clear, hard, tough, glossy, no seams*

Soft drink, water and vegetable oil bottles, washing-up liquid and liquid soap bottles, honey, peanut butter and pickle jars

**2 HDPE**

*Strongly coloured, matte (not shiny) stiff and waxy*

Milk, juice, liquid detergent, shampoo and household cleanser bottles, most shopping and rubbish bags

**3 PVC**

*Strong, smooth, resistant to oil, grease and chemicals*

Clear food and non-food trays and bottles, cling film

**4 LDPE**

*Light, often see-through, stretchy, easy to seal with heat*

Bread, frozen vegetable and dry cleaning bags, shrink wrap

**5 PP**

*Hard, smooth, cannot scratch*

Screw on caps, ketchup and medicine bottles, yoghurt, ice-cream and margarine tubs, woven plastic sacks

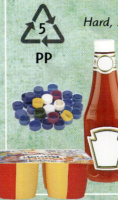

**6 PS**

*Light, fluffy, stiff, snaps easily*

Takeaway plates, tubs and cups and lids, meat trays, egg boxes, hot drink cups

*Also rigid, transparent and shiny*
CD boxes and tape cases

**7 OTHER**

*Multi-layered mixed plastics*

Snack bags, biscuit wrappers

 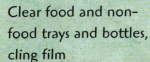

# New plastic from old

Most recycled plastic is not pure enough to be used for food and drink packaging, but it can be made into many other useful household things.

## Fine fibres

Some recycled plastic is made into stuffing for ski jackets, quilts, pillows and sleeping bags. It is also spun into thin, strong fibres used for making clothes, backpacks and carpets.

Recycled carpet **underlay**

## IT'S A FACT

Some plastic starts as a syrupy liquid and sets only once. Once it is hard, it cannot become liquid again, just like boiling an egg.

Others can melt and harden again and again, just like candle wax. Only this kind of plastic can be recycled.

25 two-litre drink bottles were needed to make this recycled fleece.

## Pots for plants

Flowerpots are often made from recycled plastic.

## Brushes and brooms

Some factories dye and pull recycled plastic into long strings. They cut the strings into short bundles to make bristles for all sorts of brushes and brooms.

Bundle of bristles

Scrubbing brush bristles

Cleaning brush bristles

Broom bristles

# Fantastic plastic

Recycled plastic can be found in unexpected places.

## Great for the garden

Recycled plastic is strong and rotproof. It is often used instead of wood or cement to make garden and park equipment, such as water butts, fencing, walkways, picnic tables and benches. It is also used for road cones, bollards and signposts.

Recycled plastic water butt

## Cool counters

Speckled recycled plastic is very decorative. People use it to make shop counters, kitchen worktops and basins.

## A curious kennel

Can you believe it?
This kennel is made with
recycled toothpaste tubes.
The plastic and aluminium
tubes are shredded into
tiny pieces, heated at a
high temperature and
pressed. The plastic bits
melt and stick to the
aluminium bits.

## Funky furniture

Designers are **experimenting** with recycled plastic
as a material for furniture. The coloured flecks
are the colours of the original plastics, all mixed up.

Rocking lounger

27

# Glossary

**bale** a large bundle

**chemicals** substances that are used to make materials

**crochet** to make stitches by twisting thread or wool around a single needle

**crude oil** a thick black liquid found under the ground or the sea

**experiment** to try out something new

**factory** a building where things are made in large numbers using machines

**fibre** a thin thread of material

**flake** a small, thin flat piece of something

**foil** a very thin sheet of metal

**granule** a small grain

**jute** a tall plant with strong stringy fibres used for bags, ropes, sacks and carpet backs

**landfill site** a huge pit in the ground where crushed rubbish is buried

**liquid** a runny substance that has no shape of its own

**material** a substance used to make something else

**mould** a block of wood, metal or other material hollowed out into the shape of an object. Melted plastic is poured into a mould to take on its shape

**natural material** a material made by nature not by people

**packaging** the protective wrapper or container for goods

**pellet** a small hard round object formed by pressing, rolling and cutting

**recycle** to use an existing object or material to make something new

**re-use** to use again

**rot** the natural way a material slowly breaks down into lots of smaller, different substances

**rust** to go brown and flaky

**underlay** a thick padding put between a floor and a carpet

# Guess what?

- About 10 per cent of the weight of your household rubbish is plastic.

- Over half the litter found on beaches is plastic.

- 6 plastic bottles weigh the same as 1 glass bottle of the same size.

- All plastics use up only 4% of the world's oil supply – the rest is used for transport and electricity.

## Useful websites

www.ollierecycles.com
A fun, interactive site for children, which includes information and tips on recycling plastics and packaging.

www.recycle-more.co.uk
Games, information and advice about recycling at home and at school, including how to find your local recycling point for plastics.

www.recoup.org
Provides the latest information about plastics recycling, downloadable factsheets and includes an on-line resources shop.

www.cleanup.com.au
An environmental action site that includes information about the problem of plastic bags and ideas for using alternatives.

# Index

bag 6, 9, 16, 18-19, 20-21, 23
beach 14, 18, 29
bollard 26
bottle 7, 8, 10, 11, 13, 15, 22, 23, 24
bottle cap 11, 13, 14, 15, 23
bristles 25
brush 13, 25
bucket 6, 9

carpet 24
CD 10, 12, 23
chemical 8
clothes 24
container 6, 11,
crochet 20

factory 8, 21, 22, 25
fibre 6, 24
flake 22
fleece 24
furniture 27

granule 8

jewellery 15

landfill site 10, 14

mould 8, 9

oil 8, 29

packaging 10, 11, 16, 22, 24
pellet 22
plastic
  making 8-9
  melting 8, 22, 24
  names/numbers 23
  recycling 11, 16, 21, 22-23, 24-25, 26-27
  re-using 10, 11, 12-13, 19
  types 22, 23
  waste 14

plastic sheet 6, 9, 21
plastic tube 6, 8, 9

record 12
road cone 26

stuffing 24

toothpaste tube 27

water butt 26
wrapper 16, 17, 23